We Will Not Cancel Us
And Other Dreams of Transformative Justice

adrienne maree brown
Afterword by Malkia Devich Cyril

W9-AXG-552

EMERGENT STRATEGY SERIES

Praise for **We Will Not Cancel Us**

"This book offers much needed ground for those of us who 'are in the mud together' as Black feminists, abolitionists, co-strugglers, and everyday people. Through her own vulnerability, adrienne maree brown invites us to ask ourselves uncomfortable questions, to name our fears and terrors ... *We Will Not Cancel Us* acknowledges humanity while inviting us to become more discerning, loving, and rigorous for the sake of collective liberation." —Charlene A. Carruthers, author of *Unapologetic: A Black, Queer, and Feminist Mandate for Radical Movements*

"As someone who wrote 'kill your rapist' on every surface I could find in the 90s and then went on to find other nonviolent solutions for transformation, *We Will Not Cancel Us* brings me face to face with my innermost conflicts about transformative justice. How do we align anger, **believing and supporting** survivors, with a values-based daily practice of accountability for those who harm us? ... In this book, adrienne maree brown gives us the space to sit with our discomfort and honors our process as growing abolitionists. She gives us points to struggle with so that we can continue on our journey to the next best version of our community, our practice, our politics, and ourselves." —Shira Hassan, co-author of *Fumbling Towards Repair: A Workbook for Community Accountability Facilitators*

"adrienne maree brown urges us to go deep, sink down, struggle, and swim as we find language, spirit, ourselves, and each other in this time of chaos. I cannot say how grateful I am for this work of poetry and love that makes sense of my/our everyday state of confusion and shows us how we might *live abolition*—not as an absolute state but as a dynamic motion forward and together." —Mimi Kim, California State University, Long Beach

"This piece is part vulnerable inquiry, part loving challenge. adrienne risks in revealing both her unthinkable thoughts and the process of public grappling. Through this, she invites all of us into authentic reflection of our practices towards accountability and our commitments in them to both life and healing." —Prentis Hemphill, movement facilitator and former Healing Justice Director at Black Lives Matter Global Network

"Do we want to practice a politic of construction or destruction? This is the fundamental question adrienne maree brown is asking in this provocative and necessary book ... She calls for radical and compassionate rigor in acknowledging, facing, and challenging how we deal with harm and hurt. I believe principled struggle is a skill and politic to be trained in—adrienne inspires us to continue creating new forms of accountability that are not punitive like the state we seek to abolish. Transformative Justice is a living practice towards the new world we want to create." —Cindy Wiesner, Grassroots Global Justice Alliance and Rising Majority

We Will Not Cancel Us: And Other Dreams of Transformative Justice
Emergent Strategy Series No. 3
© 2020 adrienne maree brown
Afterword © 2020 Malkia Devich Cyril
"We are Still Beginning" was first published in adrienne maree brown's
Emergent Strategy: Shaping Change, Changing Worlds in the chapter titled
"Resilience: How We Recover and Transform" and a similar version
appeared as "What Is/Isn't Transformative Justice?" in Ejeris Dixon and
Leah Lakshmi Piepzna-Samarasinha's edited collection *Beyond Survival:
Strategies and Stories from the Transformative Justice Movement*

ISBN: 9781849354226
E-ISBN: 9781849354233
Library of Congress Control Number: 2020942519

AK Press	AK Press
370 Ryan Avenue #100	33 Tower St.
Chico, CA 95973	Edinburgh EH6 7BN
USA	Scotland
www.akpress.org	www.akuk.com
akpress@akpress.org	akuk@akpress.org

Please contact us to request the latest AK Press distribution catalog, which features books, pamphlets, zines, and stylish apparel published and/or distributed by AK Press. Alternatively, visit our websites for the complete catalog, latest news, and secure ordering

Cover design by Herb Thornby
Printed in the United States of America on acid-free paper

Contents

INTRODUCTION
Building Abolitionist Movements

"Abolition is about presence, not absence. It's about building life-affirming institutions."
—**Ruth Wilson Gilmore**

Abolitionists know that the implications of our visions touch everything—everything must change, including us. In order to generate a future in which we all know we can belong, be human, and be held, we must build life-affirming institutions, including our movements.

This booklet, centered around an edited version of my July 2020 blog post "Unthinkable Thoughts: Call Out Culture in the Age of Covid-19," has emerged slowly, piece by piece, as I have felt a punitive tendency root and flourish within our movements. I have felt us losing our capacity to distinguish between comrade and opponent, losing our capacity to generate belonging. I share this writing with the intention of intervention and invitation.

I am reminded of the pamphlets and booklets that my teacher Grace Lee Boggs published, specific pieces of writing that she wanted people to hold in their hands and use to spark their own conversations, reckon with their relationship to the revolutionary content within. That is also my intention here—there are quite possibly more questions than answers in here, but these are conversations I hope we are all having with our own political home communities.

Every piece of writing in this book changed me in the writing of it, and scared me when I wrote it. Each of these pieces bubbled up, woke me up in the dark, tried slipping unsubtly into other writing efforts, wanted to be written. I tried to avoid being the person to write each one—I don't know all the answers. I hold space for movement growth, and every time humans are present, so is conflict, and all manner of harmful human behavior.

You are able to read these thoughts because it is my fractal responsibility to be honest about what I am seeing and feeling as patterns within our shared work. I am a tiny cell within multiple movement bodies for justice and abolition. This booklet is a bid for our movements to attend to the spiritual work of abolition in ourselves, in our movements, in the world. Emergent strategy suggests that we must work hard at getting abolitionist practice functional at a small scale so that large-scale abolition and transformative justice are more visible, rootable, possible.

We are seeding the future, including our next systems of justice, with every action we take; the fractal nature of our sacred design teaches us that our smallest choices today will become our next norms. I am concerned with what that looks like with conflict resolution and accountability within movement.

Who is the I, the We?

It always feels important to me to reveal who I am as the author of these ideas, and the lineage I draw upon.

I am a Black biracial queer fat survivor, witch, movement facilitator, and mediator. I am a student of complexity. I am learning complexity from the inside out. I am a student of change and a student of how groups change together—change themselves and change the world.

I have spent most of my political life honing the skill of neutrality. This doesn't mean my politics have ever been neutral, but that I have often held my thoughts and opinions to myself, ceding the realm of content to the communities I serve.

Because I am discerning about who I will work for, I am rarely out of alignment with the communities I serve. I have chosen to hold people whose work, and whose politics, I believe in—primarily Black and Brown organizers fighting for social and environmental justice, specifically those who are openly anti-capital-ist, feminist, Indigenous and/or following Indigenous leadership, and abolitionist. I have supported them to hash out the distinctions, positions, disagreements, and misalignments, to find their own solidarities, and be able to step forward together towards a future we are co-creating.

There are many things I do not know, am not expert in. I try not to write, speak, or be seen as a teacher in those things. Part of what happens when you become more well known is that people begin to ask you about things you don't know, expect you to know everything… And in this age of 24/7 punditry, there are a lot of gen-eralists who take up space with what they don't know, or only know a little bit about. That brief, surface-level expertise is a pet peeve of mine—I'd rather know what I know and point to others who know what I don't know.

I have studied the work of Sojourner Truth, Ange-la Y. Davis, Ruth Wilson Gilmore, Mariame Kaba, Mimi Kim, Rachel Herzing, Ron Scott, Walidah Imarisha, Shira Hassan, Ejeris Dixon, Leah Lakshmi Piepzna-Samarasinha, Mia Mingus, Mark-Anthony Johnson, Andrea Ritchie, Patrisse Cullors, and Prentis

Hemphill, among others. Much of their work has spoken of the carceral state as it relates to sexual, physical, domestic, and other commons arenas of abuse and harm. They have helped me understand the omnipresence of punitive justice—from the corporal punishment of children at home and school, to suspension, expulsion, juvenile detention in educational systems, to the imprisonment and execution of adults. They helped me see the ways that our current justice system roots into slavery: lynchings, whipping, chains, bars, police, snitches, and, in some ways the most violent punishment for an interconnected species, the removal of humans from community.

These teachers also helped me see the limitations of restorative justice—that it often meant restoring conditions that were fundamentally harmful and unequal, unjust. If the racialized system of capitalism has produced such inequality that someone is hungry and steals a purse to resource a meal, returning the purse with an apology or community service does nothing to address that hunger. These teachers brought me to transformative justice, the work of addressing harm at the root, outside the mechanisms of the state, so that we can grow into right relationship with each other.

Another dynamic occurs when people begin to see you as a teacher—you have to be more careful with your questions, with your emotional explorations…they might emerge from you as inquiry and land with another as gospel. The tricky bit here is that some of what I know best are questions—the questions a group needs to reckon with. Identifying and asking the questions doesn't mean I know the answers. In my emotional inquiries, it usually means I feel lost, and longing for a clarity that aligns with my vision of transformation from a rigid, punitive, disconnected society to an adaptive, resilient, and interdependent one.

With each of the pieces in this collection, my goal is to bring transformative justice to life *within* our movement spaces—not as a futurist theory we are demanding from the larger world, but as a practice we are rigorously in with each other as believers, growing the capacity to invite others into.

I honor all our different attempts at learning to do justice ourselves.

I respect and learn from righteous anger, my own and others.[1]

I want to punish people too sometimes, especially those whom I have survived. I'm not above it.

I don't want to protect those who cause harm, or limit the options of survivors. I want healing for all.

---

1   Check out Lama Rod Owens, *Love and Rage: The Path of Liberation Through Anger* (Berkeley: North Atlantic Books, 2020).

I want to bring our attention to patterns that echo and generate harm for survivors *and* harm doers.

I want to bring our attention to what generates healing for those survivors who receive *and* those who cause harm…and the majority, who do both.

I want to bring our attention to the things we don't yet know how to do.

I want to ask us all to commit to abolitionist practice together.

I also want to be as brave as those I look up to, those I call teacher. Many of them were willing to speak up when they felt their beloved movements heading in regressive, divisive, or capitalist directions, offering perspective and risking belonging, in order to offer some love.

This booklet is full of love notes and hopefully some clear invitations in new direction.

One Teacher from Nature

Mushrooms are a great teacher in this recentering work. One of our oldest ancestors, mycelium/mushrooms show us that the instance of life we can witness, the mushroom, is always evidence of a much more complex and wider network of connections underground. The same thing is true with conflict and harm—we are all connected to each other, at our best and at our worst.

The instances of visible dissonance, harm, and abuse in movement are evidence of toxicity in our intersecting systems of identity, belonging, resource, power, and home. One toxic substance is supremacy, so ubiquitous that it has long been invisible to those benefiting from it and can seem desirable to those suffering from it. It manifests as white supremacy, male supremacy, ableist supremacy, straight supremacy, cis supremacy, and more—the belief that some of us are normal, are better, are justified to take and do whatever we want, including harm each other and the earth.

We won't end the systemic patterns of harm by isolating and picking off individuals, just as we can't limit the communicative power of mycelium by plucking a single mushroom from the dirt. We need to flood the entire system with life-affirming principles and practices, to clear the channels between us of the toxicity of supremacy, to heal from the harms of a legacy of devaluing some lives and needs in order to indulge others.

Mycelium looks much the same way our brains look; networks of data, communication, nourishment flowing in every direction. Mycelium can help us learn how to process conflict and harm into life and beauty. Mycelium helps us see ourselves.

For the pieces in this booklet, I considered working

with the metaphors of mushrooms, or swarms of wasps, packs of hyena, zombified ants, piranha. Initially, I chose to look directly at our own behavior, because we, too, are networked nature. I looked at metaphors from human history that demonstrate ways that we are unique amongst every other species we know in terms of how we reason and communicate, but stay committed to gleeful vengeance and collective punishment. But in this booklet I have upgraded those metaphors and included explanation as to why.

I am asking you now, in this introduction, to keep on your mycelial glasses as you move through the text. Feel for any and all teachers in nature who can help us learn what we do not yet know.

To What End?

What moved me to publish these pieces in this way is that, more than anything, I want to invite us to get excellent at being in conflict, which is a healthy, natural part of being human and biodiverse. And I want us to help end the cycles of harm for Black and Brown people, which, in the spirit of the Combahee River Collective, necessitates ending these cycles for everyone.

I know that ending harm may be far off yet, even unimaginable, but I also believe that the future is already alive in each of us, because all the generations to come live within the bodies, cultures, dreams, and shaping of those alive today. I believe a future where harm is the anomaly is already rooting in our communities. I know that we are co-creating the future with each word, each action, and with our attention.

I have a vision that movements for social and environmental justice, particularly the Black and Brown formations within these larger movements, become living models of abolition. But first we have to find the rigor to fight fair, struggle in principled ways, and practice accountability beyond punishment with each other.

I can see it—in the short-term we generate small pockets of movement so irresistibly accountable that people who don't even know what a movement is come running towards us, expecting that they will be welcomed, flawed and whole, by a community committed to growth; knowing that there is a place in this violent, punitive world that is already committed to, and practicing, a healing and transformative iteration of justice. As Maurice Moe Mitchell said, we have to have a low bar for entry and a high standard for conduct.

In my mid-term vision, movements prioritize building the capacity, skill and wide hearts to receive new comrades, while practicing daily and deeply what it means to sustain our relationships and collective visions, uphold our values, and adapt towards purpose. We find ways to bond that aren't limited to pettiness, gossip, cliquishness, which can be so fun and then so destructive. We get skilled at critique that deepens us, conflict that generates new futures, and healing that changes material conditions.

In the longest term vision I can see, when we, made of the same miraculous material and temporary limitations as the systems we are born into, inevitably disagree, or cause harm, we will respond not with rejection, exile, or public shaming, but with clear naming of harm; education around intention, impact, and pattern breaking; satisfying apologies and consequences; new agreements and trustworthy boundaries; and lifelong healing resources for all involved.

I have a vision of movement as sanctuary. Not a tiny perfectionist utopia behind miles of barbed wire and walls and fences and tests and judgments and righteousness, but a vast sanctuary where our experiences, as humans who have experienced and caused harm, are met with centered, grounded invitations to grow.

In this sanctuary we feel our victory, where winning means a mass and intimate healing.

Where winning isn't measured by anyone else's loss, but by breaking cycles of abuse, harm, assault, and systemic oppression.

Where winning is measured not just by the absence of patterns of harm, distrust, and isolation, but by the presence of healing and healthy interdependence.

Where we are skilled at being honest, setting and honoring boundaries, giving and receiving apologies, asking for help, and changing our behaviors.

Where, every day, we can access the feeling of ease in our guts and calm in our jaws and shoulders.

Where we have trust deep enough to grow from conflict, trust that good intentions can yield good practice and radically reduce, even eliminate, harm. Where we trust that we are in such regular practice that we no longer have to be vigilant, to police or punish within our communities.

Holding this vision inside of movements right now has meant feeling not just for what is punitive, but for where there is gleeful othering, revenge, or punishment of others, particularly when these things deepen our belonging to each other, usually briefly, until we too fuck up.

It means paying attention to where we feel and/or practice policing and surveillance outside of the state.

It has meant longing for more collective clarity on what we mean by conflict, what we mean by harm, and what we mean by abuse. We need to get more precise about the language we use collectively.

It has meant listening for what healing is needed, and how we can become a generation that learns to be satisfied in our healing.

It has meant slowing down our initial collective reactions such that violence is not met with more violence, but with alternative and satisfying consequences that result in the reduction of harm.

It has meant feeling for what is out of alignment with abolition, for what feels like transformative justice, for what feels like radical love in action.

In order for our movements to be rooted in love, we need to be able to have conversations as survivors, thinkers, workers, and shapers of the future, where all of our experiences can feed our learning. Abolition is the idea that resonates the most to me, both as a survivor who wants to break cycles of harm and as a human who wants to belong to my species, to my planet, to my time in the journey of evolution.

It is our time and responsibility to try something else.

Gratitudes:

Thanks you to Malkia Devich Cyril and Shira Hassan for initial feedback. Thank you to all of the readers who reached out to offer their vulnerability around how these writings moved them. Thank you to transformative justice OGs who let me know this was important ground to explore. Thank you to those who engaged in direct critique with me around this piece, particularly Maryse Mitchell-Brody, Emi Kane, Ejeris Dixon—I am better for your critical feedback, for helping me understand my/our growing edges. Thank you to Mia Herndon, Sage Crump, Nalo Zidan, Toshi Reagon, Dani McClain, Jodie Tonita, Janine de Novais, and especially Autumn Brown for holding me in this unfolding learning experience.

BRINGING ABOLITION HOME
Learning and Untangling in Public

When I was writing "Unthinkable Thoughts: Call-Out Culture in the Age of Covid-19," the next piece in this collection, I felt clear about the distinctions I wanted to make, the invitation I wanted to make to movement:

- Can we hold each other, as the systems that weaken and distort our humanity crumble?

- Can we release our binary ways of thinking of good and bad in order to collectively grow from mistakes?

- Can we be abolitionist with each other?

- Can we be principled and discerning in movement conflict?

I had people I trust read it beforehand, and when I pressed "publish" I felt scared of what might come, but also faithful…that every word was the most accurate one I knew for the feeling I was trying to express, that people would understand my intentions.

The initial waves of feedback, and the overwhelming majority of feedback, has been gratitude and affirmation. I have received so many messages and testimonials from people in sectors of movement that feel seen in the piece and saddened by the quickness with which we turn against each other, troubled by our apparent collective excitement when we attack each other. The feedback came from long-term organizers, facilitators, people who identify as survivors, and as those who have caused harm, and as both, as neither. Some of it was public, and some of it was texts from comrades I hadn't heard from in a while. I exhaled—what I felt was not just in my head or within an isolated crew.

My publisher said, let's get this in print! I was excited to pull together a little book that gives us more options, more patience, more kindness, and space for healing together.

But then a second wave of feedback came. From other survivors. And, as I listened, I felt defensive (did you read the whole piece?), dismissed (don't you know I am an abolitionist survivor? don't you know how much abuse intervention I have been a part of?), hurt (why are you coming at me like this?) and, finally, curious: what am I not seeing? Not hearing? What do I not know? What can I learn?

I asked more people for feedback, and have had conversations, emails, text threads. I have learned a lot more about some things I thought I knew; heard a lot of stories, gossip, and context that people assumed I already knew because my name is reaching further than I can track; learned that so many more people are struggling with call outs in this moment than I had any idea about, and some of them felt helped by my writing, while others felt offended. I have learned how, in certain communities, the piece exacerbated existing tensions I wasn't fully aware of. I got clearer on what parts were triggers for people, what parts are political disagreement, and what parts are both. I homed in on what is within my expertise, and reaffirmed that celebrity activism is not my jam.

Here are some things I am learning:

- I need to be much clearer in my distinctions between harm and abuse. As someone who has experienced both, I was reminded of how important it was to me that my abuse be acknowledged as what it was, not reframed into a lesser impact. How important it was that I be allowed total boundaries, space for rage, space for healing, how much I needed assurance that it wasn't my fault, and that it wasn't my job to make sure those who abused and/or harmed me got their healing together. But as I have moved away from that period of my own life, I have gotten comfortable with the catch-all language of *harm* and *harm doers*, which blurs the danger and impact. Part of my critique of the way call outs are being used is that not liking someone, social media offenses, power misuse in work settings, movement conflict, and sexual assault are all getting the same level of public response. But even in that critique, I collapsed all these distinct experiences into one word: harm. I am sorry for the pain and erasure I know that caused to other survivors, and in this booklet I work to really pull these distinctions apart as clearly as I know how.

- I will make better use of content and trigger warnings.

- I explored my argument with language that felt precise to me, and within my right to use as a Black witch. It is also language that has been weaponized against communities I love, by people I am not politically aligned with, and I am earnestly looking for other metaphors to work with.

- I don't know how we get from here to there. I don't know if we have what it takes right now to support survivors while also holding an abolitionist lens, and it isn't fair on my part not to make that apparent gap clear. Those who are expert in holding domestic violence, intimate partner violence, rape support, and other skilled areas will have to lead in that realm of abolition, in part by pointing all of us towards the skills we need to develop in order to actually take on community accountability. The hopeful news is that we have the teachers... But will we prioritize learning? And how do we not drop long-haul survivor support along the way?

- I do believe deeply in the power of mediation in instances of conflict, within movements, and including interpersonal conflict. I believe it works because I have held it, been held in it, and have seen movements benefit from having people experience principled struggle with each other, set necessary boundaries, request and receive authentic and adequate apologies and continue to be committed to something larger than themselves.

- I have to be very intentional as I gain more followers. While I did not seek fame or ask for any pedestals, I can't deny that more people are taking my words seriously. And that is a privilege. I am not taking down the original blog post, because I think more can be learned from keeping it up and being transparent in what I am learning—I know I am not learning in solitude, and I hope the process helps others learn. I did commit to not putting it in print without adaptations that reflect my learning, and hope that is what you see in the piece that follows. I see all of this as a larger process of exploring abolition as an emergent strategy, and a longer multi-voice project around that will be coming out in the next year or two. I am not alone in that exploration.

- Some learning needs to be face to face, heart to heart, or at minimum thoroughly expressed. I am excited for the conversations I am in as a result of the piece, and I feel so much possibility on the horizon around how we get good at conflict and turn and face the harm and abuse rampant in our movement communities, learn to be in the complex work of abolition and survival, and actually transform the systems that hurt us into systems that hold us and allow us to heal.

Principled Struggle, Harm, Conflict, and Other Terms Used Here

"Unthinkable Thoughts: Call-Out Culture in the Age of COVID-19" was written as an emotional inquiry—having been away on sabbatical for half a year and returned, it felt so clear to me that our movements are in danger because we don't know how to handle conflict or how to move towards accountability in satisfying and collective ways. It feels like we don't know how to belong to each other, to something big and collective and decolonizing.

We are not engaging in principled struggle, and we desperately need to be.

In a nutshell, principled struggle is when we are struggling for the sake of something larger than ourselves and are honest and direct with each other while holding compassion.[1] It is when we take responsibility for our own feelings and actions and seek deeper understanding before responding (by asking questions, or reading the referenced materials). It is when we consider that a given organization, formation, or space may or may not be the space to hold what we need to bring, and that side conversations within that space should be

1 Principled struggle is a Marxist conflict framework brought into Black movement spaces most recently by N'Tanya Lee.

for the sake of better understanding rather than checking out of the work.

When we aren't mindful about principled struggle, we can end up caught in the kind of reductionist group-think that proliferates online but is rooted in, and heightens, our offline discomfort with generative conflict in cases of disagreement and difference, and community accountability/transformative justice in cases of harm and abuse.

I received a flood of grateful responses to the piece. So many people unveiled the ways they'd either been called out or participated in call outs they later felt were ungrounded, or were grounded but didn't actually stop or change the problem. I heard about how often things are turned into public campaigns of shaming and humiliation before it is even clear if the thing is a misunderstanding, mistake, contradiction, conflict, harm, or abuse. I heard gratitude from people who wanted their humanity restored, and people who want our movements to practice principled struggle and grow our skill at accountability.

But I also received critiques that both shook and grew me. I want to name the critiques clearly. The version of the piece I include in this booklet is vastly different from what I originally posted on my blog, hopefully in ways that show what I have learned so far. It is different because the critiques both helped me grasp what is confused within movement spaces, where we need to be more precise, where my language was getting in the way of the conversation, what my role is/isn't, and where I might be of use.

A question I take very seriously and am always working to be accountable around, is: who am I to be writing these things? As a non-therapist, can I speak on abuse? As a Black mixed-race woman, can I use metaphors of Black historical experience? As a facilitator, can I speak on movement drama? Are there topics I should never publicly explore? Where are the places I might detract attention from more worthy voices because of the way celebrity culture works? Am I using my privileges without clear intention? Am I exploiting my oppression?

As best practice, in my work I name where I enter the conversation, my identity and lineage, to give agency and data to you as a reader. Given where I enter, I might be who you want to hear from, I might not. I don't want to pretend that my perspective is, should be, or could ever be universal. Entering the conversation on call-out culture, I come as a facilitator, mediator, writer, Black mixed-race woman, queer survivor, visionary thinker, healer, doula, and someone dedicated first and foremost to healthy movements that can transform the injustices of our times. I am not an academic, a historian, a psychotherapist, a researcher. I share what I learn through experiences and experiments in and with communities I support. I do not, cannot, see myself through anyone else's lens, but I can listen to what others experience, balance it with my heart, and widen, focus my view. I welcome your critiques when I am being unaccountable, or less precise than is appropriate for the content at hand—and I want you to know that whatever mistakes I am still making in these pages, in these years, are not without massive effort to do the absolute best I can do. I will not be perfect, I will keep learning. I will also not be silent, I will keep learning.

So, the critiques. [TRIGGER WARNING] The most consistent critique was about the metaphors I chose to work with—suicidal ideation, lynching, and witch trials. I felt the risk of using this language in my initial writing; the risk was part of what made the thoughts unthinkable to me—I know these to be dramatic terms. And I fear that the energy in movement right now is on the spectrum of drama and violence. But the terms both triggered readers and, read literally, felt unnecessarily hyperbolic. Feeling hopeless is not being actively suicidal. Losing Internet status, a job, reputation, or even a community is not being hung, burned at the stake, or otherwise killed. I apologize to those I triggered and offended. I apologize for reaching for the low hanging fruit of these dramatic metaphors when there are other ways to speak of mob energy that are less inflammatory, based in nature, and accurate without being incendiary. The piece included here is rewritten with metaphors that feel more appropriate to the conversation, I believe, without diminishing the impact. I am particularly grateful to my sister Autumn for helping me find and generate alternate metaphors where I felt stuck in the most dramatic language.

The other most common complaint is that I collapse conflict, harm, and abuse. And that in doing so, I risk giving abusers a way to avoid accountability and risk silencing survivors who need to shed light on their abusers in order to heal and move towards safety.

There are a few reasons why this collapse happened that have become clear to me in the many conversations I have had with comrades about the piece since posting it.

One is that, as a facilitator and mediator, I often have to hold all of these in the same moment, or group, and see that the people within the circumstances don't necessarily have clarity on what exactly they are engaged in. I have seen people shift their idea of what is happening from conflict to abuse or vice versa in the midst of a conversation. Regardless of what is happening, my role is the same—how do we move forward, given the presence of this breakdown? Do we need boundaries, apologies, clarity, new protocol, a public statement, or just to get things off our chests? Sometimes it is very important that I am clear on the specifics of what's happening, but often I notice that there can be resolution and a way forward without a ton of history and detail. It is for the participants to hold their stories, and for me to step back and see the patterns, look for the portal we can pass through to the next phase of work, relationship, growth. I focus on what is needed in the moment, and what is most accountable to the collective. That sometimes looks like slowing down, stopping, and other times like finding outside support or help, or having a person leave a group or experience. Whether I'm holding space solo or with others, I often find that we aren't working on categorizing the breakdown as much as understanding the immediate individual and long-term collective needs.

As I was writing the piece, part of my issue was that our collective response to...everything...is collapsed. Call outs elicit both a consistent negative and dismissive energy, and a pleasurable take-down activation, regardless of what the call out is addressing. It has started to feel like every kind of dissonance in movements is understood through a lens of violence, abuse, and victimization. I believe that my collapse of these distinct but interconnected states of breakdown between people is indicative of a collapse of these states and needs within movement. We are in the mud together.

I have written before that we are in the very infantile stages of learning how to be in transformative justice practices with each other, to be abolitionist in real time, because we are still beginning, but the crises are so big, urgent, and constant that there is some leapfrogging, rushing ahead of ourselves, ahead of understanding a clear shared framework, clear distinctions.

Naming this, I am committing to getting more clarity on these distinctions and inviting others into deeper clarity alongside me. I asked a lot of people in various sectors of movement and healing work for an existing glossary and was unable to find a clear or easy to access tool that makes the distinctions. This doesn't mean it isn't out there. And I am not the person to create such a tool. In lieu of such a tool, I will just be clearer about what I mean in my own writing, and work to be precise throughout this booklet. Here's how I am using these terms:

ABUSE: behaviors (physical, emotional, economic, sexual, and many more) intended to gain, exert, and maintain power over another person or in a group. When abuse is present, professional support, space, and boundaries are needed.

CONFLICT: disagreement, difference, or argument between two or more people. Can be personal, political, structural. There may be power differences, and there will most likely be dynamics of privilege and oppression at play. Conflicts can be direct and named, or indirect and felt. Conflicts rooted in genuine difference are rarely resolved quickly and easily. Conflicts can be held in relationship and/or group through naming both the differences and the impact of the differences, facing the roots of the issues, and honest conversation, especially supported conversation such as mediation.

HARM: the suffering, loss, pain, and impact that can occur both in conflict and in instances of abuse, as well as in misunderstandings steeped in differences of life experience, opinion, or needs. Harm is what needs healing—working with individual healers, therapists, and in community to understand where the hurt is and what it would look like to not be ruled by it.

A few other things to name here that are also in the mix of collapsed language and energy (both in my writing and in movements I support):

CRITIQUE: an analysis or assessment of someone's work or practices. Critique ideally helps us grow collectively by detailed engagement with what comes into the public sphere as writing, creation, behavior. Critiques can help us grow and transform that which can be shaped (though I am not interested in critiques centered on aspects of people that they do not control and can't change). Critique doesn't need resolution but acceptance and discernment—you won't please everyone, take what can grow you and keep it moving. Critiques are part of how we sharpen each other.

CONTRADICTION: the presence of ideas, beliefs, or aspects of a situation that are opposed to one another. Movements are often tense with the contradiction between what we believe and are fighting for and what we feel we must practice to navigate current conditions. One example of a common contradiction in movements is our belief in climate catastrophe and environmental justice, while still believing that we need to come together physically in ways that entail massive amounts of plane rides, high levels of waste at gatherings, and unclear protocols around recycling, composting, not using plastic, and other basic environmental practices. Another contradiction is to be an abolitionist but call for the arrest of those who hurt us. Contradictions can be handled by widening our perspective, acknowledging that these oppositional truths co-exist.[2]

MISUNDERSTANDING: incorrectly interpreting or not understanding what is being communicated. Something that can be resolved through a clarifying conversation, and if not addressed, can fester into conflict.

MISTAKES: when someone straight up messes up. Says something offensive or triggering, mishandles a situation, is dishonest, has a negative impact in spite of positive intentions, or doesn't think something through. Mistakes can be resolved with an authentic, informed apology.[3]

Movements can end up in major conflicts that, had they been caught at the moment of misunderstanding, could have been resolved or avoided. Movements can end up trying to be publicly accountable for instances

---

2 A lot of my learning around contradictions is rooted in a somatic understanding of the constant presence of contradictions as a human condition. I learned this with generative somatics and Black Organizing for Leadership and Dignity.

3 I highly recommend checking out Mia Mingus's "The Four Parts of Accountability: How to Give a Good Apology," available on her blog: leavingevidence.wordpress.com/2019/12/18/how-to-give-a-good-apology-part-1-the-four-parts-of-accountability.

of abuse, harm, or conflict that are personal and require a longer term healing practice than our organizations are equipped to provide.

I want to name all of these here because I think they are all part of what is getting collapsed and miscommunicated. In my vision of healthy movements, we are able to easily communicate about whether we are in a conflict or misunderstanding, if we are uncomfortable with how others are navigating contradictions, if we have or are receiving a critique, whether harm has happened or is happening, and whether we are witnessing or experiencing abuse.

I want to learn to wield these words both as informed, practiced terms that mean something and as felt distinctions in how I and other facilitators and mediators hold movements.

UNTHINKABLE THOUGHTS
Call-Out Culture in the Age of Covid-19

What do we do with unthinkable thoughts?

Who are we in our unthinkable thinking moments?

How do we adapt together if the clues to our next pivot are unthinkable?

Maybe sharing these unthinkable thoughts will help?

I'll start with the scariest unthinkable thought for me, which is that maybe we as a species are in a state of apocalyptic fatigue—exhausted in the face of all the changes and endings we are living through. Our current collective circumstances require us to think about death, to grieve, and to consider that everything we have known has to change or come to an end. And long before this pandemic, we in the U.S. have had to live with leadership that protected our right to shoot each other, authorized state killing of citizens in our streets, in our homes, and denied every move to intervene on the climate catastrophe we have helped produce.

In the past, I have lost my connection to life, to wanting to live, thought it didn't much matter if I was here or not, and so it didn't much matter how I treated myself or others. When I was in that phase of ambiguous commitment to life, I took risks with my mind and body that I couldn't imagine taking now. I practiced cynicism and hopelessness, as if they were the measures of humor, of intelligence. It was a brief phase of my life, but during that time I believed in nothing.[1]

It "seemed easier to just swim down" in that place.[2]

I have had to choose life from deep within me. That's why I'm still here. I want to live. I want to want to live. **I think everyone chooses each day to move towards life or away from it, though some don't realize that they are making the choice. Capitalism makes it hard to see your own direction.**

I am writing this in July 2020, from within the Covid-19 pandemic. As I have watched the world respond to the pandemic, the borders between nations shift meaning in my mind. I can see which countries choose life, and which don't; which countries have a majority life-oriented citizenship, which countries/

1 Suicidal ideation shows up differently for everyone. I am trying to put my finger on a collective feeling that only feels familiar to me when I remember my own struggle here, and I do not intend to assume anyone else's experience or normalize mine.
2 Lin-Manuel Miranda, "It's Quiet Uptown," song from the second act of *Hamilton: The Musical.*

regions elect leaders who they believe will care for them;[3] which countries pivot at the highest governmental level to protect their people, to guide their people to protect themselves—places with a variety of economies and exposure have found ways to move towards life.

I wonder about the movements in those countries, what it might feel like to live and organize in a place that truly orients towards life. I don't want to romanticize any human experiment, I know each country has it's trade-offs. But what would it be like to have leadership able to admit to being wrong when new information presents itself about the dangers around and amongst us? What would it be like to organize and apply pressure to a government committed to adapting such that the majority of its citizens stay alive, rather than the stubbornness to stay the same? In our current context, it feels like movement has to push towards life against an avalanche of crisis energy that undermines a viable future.

The U.S., as a nation, does not choose, or love, life. Not in our policies, in our safety practices, in our

---

3 I am aware that anti-abortion efforts have long staked a claim on being "pro life." I want to reclaim the language of choosing and orienting towards life for a much broader framework of choices and behaviors that align with long-term human existence. I do not think we should surrender language to those who misuse and denigrate the sacred spell inside the words.

relationship to the planet and other nations. Not yet, and possibly never before.

Other nations, many amongst the most developed in the world, initially shrugged at Covid-19. Then they adapted.

The U.S. response has been more egregious than a shrug; it's been a flagrant disregard, running towards a category-five pandemic tornado. It's meant that those of us who want to live are watching in horror as the mutating coronavirus fills in the pre-existing grooves of collective hopelessness and the resistance of those who love life—with climate deniers and corporate polluters on one side, environmental and climate justice movements on the other. White supremacists and patriarchs on one side, solidarity movements in race, ethnicity, class, gender, ability, and sexuality arenas on the other.

We are a nation not just diverse or divided, but torn—pulled towards life and pulled towards death. When I get that torn feeling within, which in recent years comes very rarely, in twinges and wisps, I now recognize it as a suicidal tendency in me. It's not the truth, not the only truth, not my truth, not the choice I want to make. But the tendency is wily, using the voices of people I love to make itself heard. I have to be vigilant, listen between the lines, ask: who would benefit from my absence? Who benefits from my self-doubt?

Under our blustering exceptional patriotism, our nation has a tendency towards its own destruction, a doubt of its right to exist, which is rooted in our foundation. It's a shame-filled foundation. Can we heal all the way down to the roots of this nation, especially if it's the only way we will want to go on?

I think our movements struggle inside this larger national hopelessness and overwhelming history of trauma and shame—we are combating that which we simultaneously internalize. We want to grow, but at the same time some of us don't seem to believe we will all get there, or get anywhere better, in time. That we can't, and won't, put forth the effort.

Maybe the idea of our future generations experiencing peace and abundance is not quite enough to keep us going.

Maybe we just need some more immediate signs of life.

Maybe we are terrified.

I, we, have to be able to discern what is me/us and what is fear.

Which leads to my next unthinkable thought: do I really know the difference between my discernment and my fear?

My dear friend Malkia Devich Cyril teaches me that there is the fear intended to save your life, versus fear intended to end it. What I mean by discernment is the set of noticings, fears, wisdoms, deductions, and gut tremblings that want to save, or even just improve, my life, versus the fear that makes me unable to do anything, that makes me unable to draw on my life force to take action.

Do I think I am being discerning when I am actually frozen in place, scared to change?

Am I too scared of standing out from the crowd to pause and discern right action?

Am I acting from terror?

Am I able to discern a decision or action that makes sense?

I was in Italy when the pandemic really became clear as a threat to my well being. I froze. In my frozen state I would hear just a bit of the news, the new numbers of crisis, and shake my head at the idiots in office, and then numb back out. Having quickly identified who I blamed, I was less able to feel any agency in myself. I froze and delayed and froze until I was overwhelmed.

Then I had an excellent therapy session where I noticed:

Oh. *I am afraid.*

I am afraid that the pandemic is on the rise

everywhere and I am going to leave safety for a danger-ous unknown.

Oh!

I don't know what to do!

As soon as I acknowledged I was afraid I was able to move into discernment. My fear became data—I am afraid because the numbers are daunting and no per-fect move is available. My fear is actually screaming on behalf of my informed intuition.

My fear made me freeze until I allowed myself to feel my actual panic, my grief, my powerlessness, my limited options. Therapy helped me notice I was afraid, deepen my breath, and return to discernment.

I see the same vacillation between fear and discern-ment in our movements right now, with no therapist in sight.

We are afraid of being hurt, afraid because we have been hurt, afraid because we have caused hurt, afraid because we live in a world that wants to hurt us wheth-er we have hurt others or not, just based on who we are, on any otherness from some long-ago determined norm. **Supremacy is our ongoing pandemic. It partners with every other sickness to tear us from life, or from lives worth living.**

So we stay put and scream into the void, mov-ing our rage across the Internet like a tornado that, without discernment, sucks up all in its path for destruction.

Our emotions and need for control have been heightened during this pandemic—we are stuck in our houses or endangering ourselves to go out and work, terrified and angry at the loss of our plans and normalcy, terrified and angry at living under the oppressive rule of an administration that does not love us and that is racist and ignorant and violent. Grieving our unnecessary dead, many of whom are dying alone, unheld by us. We are full of justified rage. And we want to release that rage. And one really fast and easy way to do this is what I experience as knee jerk collective punishment in movements.

I am speaking of the social destruction of call outs and/or cancelations. Call outs have a long history as a brilliant strategy for marginalized people to stand up to those with power. Call outs have been a way to bring collective pressure to bear on corporations, institutions, and abusers on behalf of individuals or oppressed peoples who cannot stop the injustice and get accountability on their own. There are those out of alignment with life, consent, dignity, and humanity who will only stop when a light is shined onto their inhumane behavior.

But many of the call outs burning through our movements today don't feel aligned with the lineage of this tactic. Right now, call outs are being used not just as a necessary consequence for those wielding power to cause harm or enact abuse, but to shame and humiliate people in the wake of misunderstandings, contradictions, conflicts, and mistakes. I want to place my finger on the destructive power of punitive justice currently unleashed in our movements, and see how we bring abolition, vision, and skill to the wounds.

In the past week I have seen people and organizations called out for embodying white supremacy in the workplace, for causing repeated or one-time sexual harm, for physical, emotional, or digital abuse or harm, for appropriation of ideas and images, for patriarchy, for ableism, for being dishonest, for saying harmful things a decade ago, for doing things that were later understood as harm or abuse—for embodying all of the pain that supremacy holds.

The call outs generally share one side of what's happened and then call for immediate consequences. And within a day, the call out is everywhere, the cycle of blame and shame activated, and whoever was called out has begun being publicly punished. Sometimes, there are consequences—loss of job, community, reputation, platform. Sometimes there is just derision, and calls for disappearance. The details of the offense blur or compound as others add their own opinions and experiences to the story.

We don't have a collective clarity about the distinctions between conflict, harm, or abuse, but online, we seem to respond to all of it with the same energy—consistently punitive, too often joyful.

I am not speaking of survivors naming their abusers or perpetrators here—the work of a survivor is to survive, using any and all tools available to stop the abuse and pain being exacted upon them.

I am speaking about what we do when we hear of harm, abuse, or conflict—we as community members, friends, family, partners, coworkers, comrades, people engaged in our own cycles of harm and healing. As movements trying to break cycles of harm and abuse, how do we hold survivors and those who cause harm as community members once they speak up?

Currently, a wide variety of harm doing gets collapsed into one label of "bad, disposable person/organization" and receives one punishment: a call out, often for some form of instant cancelation. And in relationship, alongside of, sometimes overlapping with these cycles of naming harm and abuse, are conflicts. Our conflicts, our interpersonal disagreements, can currently get escalated into the language and response of harm and abuse.

We are afraid, and we think it will assuage our fears and make us safer if we can clarify an enemy, a someone outside of ourselves who is to blame, who is guilty, who is the origin of harm. Can we acknowledge that trauma and conflict can distort our perspective of responsibility and blame in ways that make it difficult to see the roots of the harm?

Instant judgment and punishment are practices of power over others. It's what those with power do to those who can't stop them, who can't demand justice. This injustice of power is practiced at an individual and collective level.

What concerns me is how often it feels like this instant reaction is happening within movement. It feels like a feeding frenzy. In nature, a feeding frenzy happens "when predators are overwhelmed by the amount of prey available.... This can cause [them] to go wild, biting anything that moves, including each other or anything else within biting range."[4] There is an abundance of harm, abuse, and righteous conflict surrounding us right now. But we in movement don't identify with predators—our historical reality is that we are the prey, trying to defend ourselves, protect each other. There is such complexity with trying to name this dynamic within our movements. I persist in this line of inquiry because it's also true that we are practicing,

4   Wikipedia entry for "Feeding Frenzy," https://en.wikipedia.org/wiki/Feeding_frenzy.

training ourselves through repeated motion, a strategy of moving in frenzy towards punitive actions, even as we try to put transformative language on our behavior.

How do we, in movements, become responsible for each other, accountable to a vision beyond the carceral system that will only come to pass if we practice it in the present?

This generation of movements for justice didn't create this punitive system of justice. We didn't create the state, we didn't choose to be socialized within it. We want to dismantle these systems of mass harm, and I know that most of us have no intention of ever mimicking state processes of navigating justice.

The tools of swift and predatory justice feel good to use, familiar, groove in the hand easily from repeated use and training, briefly satisfying. But these tools are often blunt and senseless.

Unless we have an analysis of abolition and dismantling systems of oppression, we will not realize what's in our hands, we will never put the predator's tools down and figure out what our tools are and can be.

My third unthinkable thought—why does it feel like we are committed to punishment, and enjoying it? Why do our movements more and more often feel like we are moving with sharp teeth against ourselves? And what is at stake because of that pattern, that feeling?

Why does it feel like someone pointing at someone else and saying: "that person is harmful!," and with no questions or process or time or breath, we are collectively punishing them, tearing them, and anyone protecting them, to shreds?

Sometimes we even do it with the language of transformative justice: claiming that we are going to give them room to grow. They need to disappear completely to be accountable. We are publicly shaming them so that they will learn to be better.

Underneath this logic I hear: we are good and we are getting rid of the "bad" people in our community or movement. We are affirming our rightness and power.

Which isn't to say that some of the accused aren't raging white supremacists in movement clothing. Or abusers who have slipped through the fingers of accountability. Or shady in some other way.

Which isn't to say that a public accounting of harm, and consequences, isn't necessarily the correct move. In cases of rape, sexual assault, intimate partner violence, and abuse, the callout can be the only move that stops the immediate harm without engaging the state. Shaming behaviors of abuse in a culture where they have been normalized is, and has been, a necessary survival technology.

Which isn't to say we don't believe survivors. Because we must. In fact, part of what inspired this piece is making room for survivors to be heard.

But how do we believe survivors and still be abolitionist? And still practice transformative justice?

To start with, I have been trying to discern when a call out feels powerful, like the necessary move, versus when it feels like a feeding frenzy.

The first and biggest thing is that call outs never feel powerful to me as a move to resolve conflict, especially when that conflict is unveiled without the consent of both or all parties in the dispute. Call outs don't work for addressing misunderstandings, issuing critiques, or resolving contradiction.

Call outs feel most powerful when they are used with their tactical intention—for those with less positional, political, economic, or other power to demand accountability to stop harm or abuse. I want to spend some time here, because even in that context, I believe we have a responsibility to be in principled struggle and transformative justice—to seek consequences in a context of ancestral, generational, and present-day trauma, to unlearn the pleasure of punishing each other with public humiliation and shame. We need to understand that each call out puts our community members, survivors, and harm doers, on the radar of a state that has a history of surveilling, infiltrating, and otherwise strategically weakening movements that are having, or could have, actual impact in changing material conditions for oppressed peoples.

Here are some questions I sit with when I am asked to engage in a call out:

- Have there been any private efforts for accountability or conflict resolution?

- Is/are the survivor(s) being adequately supported?

- Has the accused individual or group acknowledged what they've done, or are they saying something different happened, or even that nothing happened?

- Has the accused individual or group avoided accountability? Have they continued to cause harm?

- Has the accused already begun the process of taking accountability?

- Does the accused person have significantly more power than the accuser(s)—in what ways? Are they using that power to avoid accountability?

- Is this a demand for process and consequences that will satisfy the survivor, the community, the movement?

- Is this call out precise? Is the demand for accountability related to the alleged harm?

- Does it feel like we can ask questions?

- Is all the attention going towards the person accused of harm?

- Are we being asked to rush to action? Is there enough time between the accusation and the call for consequences to make sure we know what's going on and what's possible?

- Is the only acceptable consequence to those making the call out for the accused to cease to exist?

- Is the accused from one or more oppressed identities?

- Is there any discernible power difference between the accused and the accuser(s)?

• Does this feel performative?

We have to recognize that we are on dangerous territory that is not aligned with a transformative justice vision when we mete out punishments in place of consequences, and/or when we issue consequences with no inquiry, no questions, no acceptance of accountability, no process, no time for the learning and unlearning necessary for authentic change…just instant and often unsatisfactory consequences.

A moment on this: one of the main demands in call outs is for a public apology. To expect a coherent authentic apology from someone who has been forcibly removed from power or credibility feels like a set up. Usually they issue some PR-sounding thing that works like blood in the water, escalating the feeding frenzy instead of satisfying our hunger for justice.

We've all seen the convoluted, denial-accountability-nonapology message from accused harm doers, especially when physical or sexual harm is involved. Sometimes they are claiming innocence, sometimes they are admitting to some harm, rarely at the level of the accusation. Sometimes they say they tried to have a process but it didn't work, or they were denied. Who knows what they mean by process, who knows if the accuser was ready for a process, who knows what actually happened between them, the relational context of the instance or pattern of harm? Who knows?

The truth about sexual assault and rape and patriarchy and white supremacy and other abuses of power is that we are swimming in them, in a society that has long normalized them, and that they often play out intimately.

The truth is, sometimes it takes a long time for us to realize the harm that has happened to us.

And longer to realize we have caused harm to others.

The truth is, it isn't unusual to only realize harm happened in hindsight, with more perspective and politicization.

But there's more truth, too.

The additional truth is, right now, in the frantic pause of pandemic, we have the time.

The additional truth is, even though we want to help the survivor, we love obsessing over and punishing "villains." We end up putting more of our collective attention on punishing those accused of causing harm than supporting and centering the healing of survivors, and/or building pathways for those who are in cycles of causing harm to change.

The additional truth is, we want to distance ourselves from those who cause harm, and we are steeped in a punitive culture, which, right now, is normalizing a methodology of "punish first, ask questions later." And, because we are in the age of social media, we now have a way to practice very publicly.

> "Instead of asking whether anyone should be locked up or go free, why don't we think about why we solve problems by repeating the kind of behavior that brought us the problem in the first place?"
> —**Ruth Wilson Gilmore**

The other metaphor that feels deeply present in this period of call outs is cancer. Supremacy works as a collective cancer, an invisible and highly productive disease that quietly roots deep within us. We are better than… someone. We might experience supremacy due to race, citizenship, gender, class, ableism, age, access, fame, or other areas where we feel justified to cause harm without consequence. Sometimes we don't even realize we have caused harm, because supremacy is a numbing and narrowing disease.

I want us to let go of the narrowness of innocence, widen our understanding of how harm moves through us.[5] I want us to see individual acts of harm as symp-

---

5   Prentis Hemphill, "Letting Go of Innocence," Prentis Hemphill blog, prentishemphill.com/blog/2019/7/5/letting-go-of-innocence, July 5, 2019.

toms of systemic harm, and to do what we can do collectively to dismantle the systems and get as many of us free as possible.

Often a call out comes because the disease has reached an acute state in someone, is festering in hiding, is actively causing harm. I want us to see the difference between the human and the disease, to see what we are afraid of, in others and in ourselves, and discern a path that actually addresses the root of our justified fears.

This is not a case against call outs. There is absolutely a need for certain call outs—when power is greatly imbalanced and efforts have been made to stop ongoing harm, when someone accused of harm won't participate in community accountability processes or honor requested boundaries, the call out is a way of pulling an emergency brake. But call outs need to be used specifically for harm and abuse, and within movement spaces they should be deployed as a last option.

We must be able to acknowledge that we are on new ground, where the pressure of a call out is no longer localized, relational, or sector specific. Transformative justice is relational, it happens at the scale of community. Call outs now often happen at the scale of viral threads amongst strangers. The consequences of being called out in this hyper-connected age can be extremely dire and imprecise—facilitators and mediators like myself often get the call after, when someone accused of harm is struggling to stay alive after losing their reputation, community, and/or work. If we are lucky we can connect them to therapy or support community accountability. But often we are overwhelmed, and people slip through the cracks to cause harm to themselves, or leave movement and continue their abusive patterns elsewhere.

Additionally, and historically, the presence of infiltration in our movements is documented and prevalent. This also comes to those of us who facilitate movements often—the quiet whisper that someone in the meeting leaked the notes, is antagonizing without principle, appeared out of nowhere and started taking up a ton of space. The reach of COINTELPRO and subsequent surveillance and infiltration campaigns is still being uncovered, and this strategy reaches back as long as humans have waged war against each other. Call outs are an incredible modern tool for those who are not committed to movements to use against those having impact.

Right now calling someone out online seems like first/only option for a lot of people in the face of any kind of dissonance. We need to have the skills to be able to discern what kind of dissonance we are we dealing with or being asked to help with, what kind of support is actually needed, and the capacity we have to meet that need without calling on or informing the state.

Too often, we are using call outs to avoid direct conflict. Call outs are also being used to tilt public opinion about organizational or sectoral conflicts. Conflict, and growing community that can hold political difference, are actually healthy, generative, necessary moves for vibrant visions to be actualized.

I can't help but wonder who benefits from movements that engage in public infighting, blame, shame, and knee-jerk call outs? I can't help but see the state grinning, gathering all the data it needs, watching us weaken ourselves. Meanwhile, the conflicts are unresolved, and/or harm continues.

This piece is crucial to me. If the kind of call outs currently sweeping through online organizing space and spilling into real-life formations actually stopped harm, resolved conflict, ended supremacy, transformed people, I'd be a gung-ho call-out machine! I *love* functional tools. But what happens more often is that people step back, move through their shame, leave movement, or double down and return with even more egregious acts of flagrant harm and/or unprincipled struggle methods.

I long for more people to experience the satisfaction of the processes I have been in and held—not perfection, but satisfaction. People getting to name what caused hurt, where the conflict is, what is needed; people receiving an authentic apology; people getting to commit to paths of unlearning harmful belief systems and behaviors.

I don't find it satisfying, and I don't think it is transformative to publicly call people out for instant consequences with no attempt at a conversation, mediation, boundary setting, or community accountability (which often happens in a supported process with a limited number of known participants).

It doesn't make sense to say "believe all survivors" if we don't also remember that most of us are survivors, which includes most people who cause harm. What we mean is we are tired of being silenced, dismissed, powerless in our pain, hurt over and over. Yes. But being loud is different from being whole, or even being heard, being cared for, being comforted, being healed. Being loud is different from being just. Being able to destroy is different from being able to generate a future where harm isn't happening all around us.

We are terrified of how widespread and active harm is, and it makes us want to point the finger and quickly remove those we can identify as bad. We want to protect each other from those who cause harm.

Many of us seem to worry that if we don't immediately answer the feeding frenzy invitations in our DMs, that we will be next to be called out, or called a rape apologist or a white person whisperer or an internalized misogynist, or just disposed of for refusing to group-think and then group-act. Online, we perform solidarity for strangers rather than engaging in hard conversations with comrades.

We are fearful of taking the time to be discerning, because then we may have to recognize that we aren't as skilled at conflict as we want and need to be, and/or that any of us could be seen as harm-doers. When we are discerning, when we do step up to say wait, let's get understanding here, we risk becoming the new target, viewed as another accomplice to harm instead of understood as a comrade in ending harm, viewed as an opposition in conflict instead of someone trying to find movement alignment.

Perhaps, most dangerously, we are, all together now, teetering on the edge of hopelessness. Collective pandemic burnout, 45-in-office burnout, climate catastrophe burnout, and other exhaustions have us spent and flailing, especially if we are caught in reactive loops (which include the culture of multiple daily call outs) instead of purposeful adaptations. Some of us are losing hope, tossed by the tornado, ungrounded and uprooted by the pace of change, seeking something tangible we can do, control, hold, throw away.

The kind of call outs we are currently engaging in do not necessarily think about movements' needs as a whole. Movements need to grow and deepen. We need to "transform ourselves to transform the world," to "be transformed in the service of the work."[6] Movements need to become the practice ground for what we are healing towards, co-creating. Movements are responsible for embodying what we are inviting our people into. We need the people within our movements, all socialized into and by unjust systems, to be on liberation paths. Not already free, but practicing freedom every day. Not already beyond harm, but accountable for doing our individual and internal work to end harm and engage in generative conflict, which includes actively working to gain awareness of the ways we can and have harmed each other, where we have significant political differences, and where we can end cycles of harm and unprincipled struggle in ourselves and our communities.

Knee-jerk call outs say: those who cause harm or mess up or disagree with us cannot change and cannot belong. They must be eradicated. The bad things in the world cannot change, we must disappear the bad until there is only good left.

6   Grace Lee Boggs, *Living for Change: An Autobiography* (Minneapolis: University of Minnesota Press, 1998), 153; Mary Hooks, quoted in "The Mandate: A Call and Response from Black Lives Matter Atlanta," SONG website, https://southernersonnewground.org/themandate, July 14, 2016.

But one layer under that, what I hear is:

We cannot change.

We do not believe we can create compelling pathways from being harm doers to being healed, to growing.

We do not believe we can hold the complexity of a gray situation.

We do not believe in our own complexity.

We do not believe we can navigate conflict and struggle in principled ways.

We can only handle binary thinking: good/bad, innocent/guilty, angel/abuser, black/white, etc.

Cancer attacks one part of the body at a time, I have seen it—oh it's in the throat, now it's in the lungs, now it's in the bones. When we engage in knee-jerk call outs as a conflict-resolution device, or issue instant consequences with no process, we become a cancer unto ourselves, unto movements and communities. We become the toxicity we long to heal. We become a tool of harm when we are trying to be, and I think meant to be, a balm.

Oh unthinkable thoughts. Now that I have thought you, it becomes clear to me that all of you are rooted in a singular longing: I want us to want to live.

I want us to want to live in this world, in this time, together.

I want us to love this planet and this species, at this time.

I want us to see ourselves as larger than just individuals randomly pinging around in a world that will never care for us.

I want us to see ourselves as a murmuration of creatures who are, as far as we know right now, unique in all the universe. Each cell, each individual body, itself a unique part of this unique complexity.

I want us not to waste the time we have together.

I want us to look at each other with the eyes of interdependence, such that when someone causes harm, we find the gentle parent inside of us who can use a voice of accountability, while also bringing curiosity—"Why did you cause harm? Do you know? Do you know other options? Apologize." That we can set boundaries that don't require the disappearance of other survivors. That we can act towards accountability with the touch of love. That when someone falls behind, we can use a parent's voice of discipline, while also picking them up and carrying them for a while if needed.

I want us to adapt from systems of oppression and punishment to systems of uplifting and transforming.

I want us to notice that this is a moment when we need to orient and move towards life, not surrender to the incompetence and hopelessness of our national leadership.

I want us to be discerning.

I want our movement to feel like a vibrant, accountable space where causing harm does not mean you are excluded immediately and eternally from healing, justice, community, or belonging.

I want us to grow lots and lots of skill at holding the processes by which we mend the wounds in our communities and ourselves.

I want satisfying consequences that actually end cycles of harm, generate safety, and deepen movement.

I want us to have an abundance of skill in facilitation and mediation when what needs to be addressed is at the level of misunderstanding, contradiction, mistake, or conflict. I want us collectively to be able to use precise language and to be comfortable asking each other questions for the sake of providing each other the absolute best, most healing and most satisfying support possible.

Within Black movement, I want us to hold Black humanity to the highest degree of protection. Yes, even when we have caused harm. I want us to see each other's trauma-induced behavior as ancestral and impermanent, even as we hold each other accountable.

I want us to be particularly rigorous about holding

complexity and accountability well for Black people in our movement communities who are already struggling to keep our heads above water and build trust and move towards life under the intersecting weights of white supremacy, racialized capitalism, police brutality, philanthropic competition culture, and lack of healing support.

I never want to see us initiate processes for Black accountability where those who are not invested in Black life can see it, store it, weaponize it. I want us to acknowledge that the state is watching, listening, and making use of our limitations. I want us to abolish the state, including the ways we support them to dominate us. Replace Black in that sentence with any other oppressed peoples and I still feel the same way. It is not strategic, and, again, it is rarely satisfying.

I want us to ask who benefits from our hopelessness, and to deny our oppressors the satisfaction of getting to see our pain. I want them to wonder how we foment such consistent and deep solidarity and unlearning. I want our infiltrators to be astounded into their own transformations, having failed to tear us apart.

I want us to acknowledge that the supremacy and hopelessness and harm and conflict are everywhere, and make moves that truly allow us to heal into wholeness.

Because against all odds in space and time? We. Are. Winning.

We are winning in spite of the tsunami of pressures against us. We are moving towards life in spite of everything that wants us to give up.

We in movement must learn to choose life even in conflict, even when seeking accountability, composting the tension and bad behaviors while holding the beating hearts.

Moving towards life affirming movements includes asking:

- In cases of abuse or assault, what does the survivor need?

- In cases of conflict, what resolution is possible?

- What are the visible and invisible power dynamics?

- Do I have the necessary information to form an opinion?

- Do I have the time to seek understanding?

- Did a conversation/process already happen?

- Is a conversation/process possible?

- How do we be abolitionist while gaining accountability here?

- Who benefits from me doubting that our movement can hold this?

- Who could hold this well?

- What will end the cycle of harm here?

- What will help us find a way forward?

We must learn to do this before there is no one left to call out, or call we, or call us.

WE ARE STILL BEGINNING

I've been thinking a lot about transformative justice lately.

In the past few months I've been to a couple of gatherings I was really excited about, and then found myself disappointed, not because drama kicked up, which is inevitable, but because of how we, as participants and organizers and people, handled those dramas.

Simultaneously I've watched several public take-downs, call outs, and other grievances take place on social and mainstream media. Some of those have been of strangers, but recently I've had the experience of seeing people I know and love targeted and taken down. In most cases, very complex realities get watered down into one flawed aspect of these people's personalities, or one mistake or misunderstanding. A mob mentality takes over then, an evisceration of character that is punitive, traumatizing, and isolating.

This has happened with increasing frequency over the past year, such that I'm wondering if those of us with an intention of transforming the world have a common understanding of the kind of justice we want to practice, now and in the future.

What we do now is find out someone or some group has done (or may have done) something out of alignment with our values. Some of the transgressions are small—saying something fucked-up, being disrespectful in a group process. Some are massive—false identity, sexual assault.

We then tear that person or group to shreds in a way that affirms our values. We create memes, reducing someone to the laughing stock of the Internet that day. We write think-pieces on how we are not like that person, and obviously wouldn't make the same mistakes they have made. We deconstruct them as thinkers, activists, groups, bodies, partners, parents, children— finding all of the contradictions and limitations and shining bright light on them. When we are satisfied that that person or group is destroyed, we move on. Or sometimes we just move on because the next scandal has arrived, the smell of fresh meat overwhelming our interest in finishing the takedown.

I say "we" and "our" intentionally here. I'm not above this behavior. I laugh at the memes, I like the apoplectic statuses, the rants with no named target that very clearly critique a specific person. I've been examining this—why I can get caught up in a mob on the Internet in a way I rarely do in life (the positive mob mentality I participate in for, say, Beyoncé or Björk feels quite different, though I know there is something in there about belonging…eh, next book). I have noticed that at the most basic level, I feel better about myself because I'm on the right side of history… or at least the news cycle.

But lately, as the attacks grow faster and more vicious, I wonder: is this what we're here for? To cultivate a fear-based adherence to reductive common values? What can this lead to in an imperfect world full of sloppy, complex humans? Is it possible we will call each other out until there's no one left beside us?

I've had tons of conversations with people who, in these moments of public flaying, avoid stepping up on the side of complexity or curiosity because in the back of our minds is the shared unspoken question: when will y'all come for me?

I have also had experiences where I absolutely wanted to take someone down, expose them as a liar, cheater, manipulator, assailant. In each of these situations, time, conversation, and vulnerability have created other possibilities, and I have ended up glad that I didn't go that route, which is generally so short-term in its impact. Sometimes this was because transformation was possible between us. Sometimes this was because the takedown wouldn't have had the impact I wanted; destroying a person doesn't destroy all of the systems that allow harmful people to do harm. These takedowns make it seem as if massive problems are determined at an individual level, as if these individuals set a course as children to become abusers, misogynists, racists, liars.

How do I hold a systemic analysis and approach when each system I am critical of is peopled, in part, by the same flawed and complex individuals that I love? This question always leads me to self-reflection. If I can see the ways I am perpetuating systemic oppressions, if I can see where I learned the behavior and how hard it is to unlearn it, I start to have more humility as I see the messiness of the communities I am part of, the world I live in.

The places I'm drawn to in movement espouse a desire for transformative justice—justice practices that go all the way to the root of the problem and generate solutions and healing there, such that the conditions that create injustice are transformed.

A lot of people use these words, and yet…we don't really know how to do it.

We call it "transformative justice" when we're throwing knives and insults, exposing each other's worst mistakes, reducing each other to moments of failure. We call it "holding each other accountable."

I recently reposted these words from Ryan Li Dahlstrom, speaking about this trend in the queer community:

> I'm feeling really tired of the call-out culture on social media especially within queer/trans people of color communities. We need to center and build relationships with one another and not keep tearing one another down publicly without trying to have direct conversations. While there are many places of learning, growth, and contradictory practice within the world we live in, why can't we talk to one another directly and allow room for learning from our mistakes or differences? By making these public attacks on each other, we are engaging in the same disposability politics of capitalism and the prison industrial complex that we purport to be against while feeding into state surveillance tactics that are monitoring how we are tearing each other down. Enough is enough y'all. We need each other now more than ever.[1]

---

1 This quote was originally posted on Ryan Li Dahlstrom's Facebook page and is shared with permission.

Yes, Ryan Li, I too am tired of it. But I see it everywhere I turn.

When the response to mistakes, failures, and misunderstandings is emotional, psychological, economic, and physical punishment, we breed a culture of fear, secrecy, and isolation.

So I'm wondering, in a real way: How can we pivot toward practicing transformative justice? How do we shift from individual, interpersonal, and inter-organizational anger toward viable, generative, sustainable systemic change?

In my facilitation and mediation work, I've seen three questions that can help us grow. I offer them here in context with a real longing to hear more responses, to get in deep practice that helps us create conditions conducive to life in our movements and communities.

1. Why? Listen with "Why?" as a framework.

People mess up. We lie, exaggerate, betray, hurt, and abandon each other. When we hear that something bad has happened, it makes sense to feel anger, pain, confusion, and sadness. But to move immediately to punishment means that we stay on the surface of what has happened.

To transform the conditions of the "wrongdoing,"

we have to ask ourselves and each other "Why?" Even—especially—when we are scared of the answer.

It's easy to decide a person or group is shady, evil, psychopathic. The hard truth (hard because there's no quick fix) is that long-term injustice creates most evil behavior. The percentage of psychopaths in the world is just not high enough to justify the ease with which we attempt to label that condition to others.

In my mediations, "Why?" is often the game-changing, possibility-opening question. That's because the answers rehumanize those we feel are perpetrating against us. "Why?" often leads us to grief, abuse, trauma, often undiagnosed mental illnesses like depression or bipolar disorder, difference, socialization, childhood, scarcity, loneliness. Also, "Why?" makes it impossible to ignore that we might be capable of a similar transgression in similar circumstances. We don't want to see that.

Demonizing is more efficient than relinquishing our world views, which is why we have slavery, holocausts, lynchings, and witch trials in our short human history.

"Why?" can be an evolutionary question.

2. Ask yourself/selves: What can I/we learn from this?
I love the pop star Rihanna, not just because she smokes blunts in ball gowns, but because one of her earliest tattoos says, "Never a failure, always a lesson."

If the only thing I can learn from a situation is that some humans do bad things, it's a waste of my precious time—I already know that.

What I want to know is: What can this teach me/us about how to improve our humanity?

What can we learn? In every situation there are lessons that lead to transformation.

3. How can my real-time actions contribute to transforming this situation (versus making it worse)?

This question feels particularly important in the age of social media, where we can make our pain viral before we've even had a chance to feel it. Often we are well down a path of public shaming and punishment before we have any facts about what's happening. That's true of mainstream takedowns, and it's true of interpersonal grievances.

We air our dirt not to each other, but with each other, with hashtags or in specific but nameless rants, to the public, and to those who feed on our weakness and divisions.

We make it less likely to find room for mediation and transformation.

We make less of ourselves.

Again, there are times when that kind of calling out

is the only option—particularly in relation to those of great privilege who are not within our reach.

But if you have each other's phone numbers, or are within two degrees of social-media connection, and particularly if you are in the small, small percentage of humans trying to change the world—you actually have access to transformative justice in real time. Get mediation support, think of the community, move toward justice.

Real time is slower than social-media time, where everything feels urgent. Real time often includes periods of silence, reflection, growth, space, self-forgiveness, processing with loved ones, rest, and responsibility.

Real-time transformation requires stating your needs and setting functional boundaries.

Transformative justice requires us, at minimum, to ask ourselves questions like these before we jump, teeth bared, for the jugular.

I think this is some of the hardest work. It's not about pack hunting an external enemy, it's about deep shifts in our own ways of being.

But if we want to create a world in which conflict and trauma aren't the center of our collective existence, we have to practice something new, ask different questions, access again our curiosity about each other as a species.

And so much more.

I want us to do better. I want to feel like we are responsible for each other's transformation. Not the transformation from vibrant flawed humans to bits of ash, but rather the transformation from broken people and communities to whole ones. I believe transformative justice could yield deeper trust, resilience, and interdependence. All these mass and intimate punishments keep us small and fragile. And right now our movements and the people within them need to be massive and complex and strong.

I want to hear what y'all think, and what you're practicing in the spirit of transformative justice. Towards wholeness and evolution, loves.

WE WILL NOT CANCEL US

We will not cancel us.

We hurt people.

Of course we did, we are human. We were traumatized/socialized away from interdependence. We learned to hide everything real, everything messy, weak, complex. We learned that fake shit hurts, but it's acceptable.

Our swallowed pain made us a piece of shit, or depressed, or untrustworthy, or paranoid, or impotent, or an egomaniac. We moved with the herd, or became isolationist and contrary, perhaps even controversial. We disappointed each other, at the level of race, gender, species…in a vast way we longed for more from us.

But we will not cancel us.

Canceling is punishment, and punishment doesn't stop the cycle of harm, not long term. Cancelation may even be counter-abolitionist… Instead of prison bars we place each other in an overflowing box of untouchables—often with no trial—and strip us of past and future, of the complexity of being gifted and troubled, brilliant and broken. We will set down this punitive measure and pick each other up, leaving no traumatized person behind.

We will not cancel us. But we must earn our place on this earth.

We will tell each other we hurt people, and who. We will tell each other why, and who hurt us and how. We will tell each other what we will do to heal ourselves, and heal the wounds in our wake. We will be accountable, rigorous in our accountability, all of us unlearning, all of us crawling towards dignity. We will learn to set and hold boundaries, communicate without manipulation, give and receive consent, ask for help, love our shadows without letting them rule our relationships, and remember we are of earth, of miracle, of a whole, of a massive river—love, life, life, love.

We all have work to do. Our work is in the light. We have no perfect moral ground to stand on, shaped as we are by this toxic complex time. We may not have time, or emotional capacity, to walk each path together. We are all flailing in the unknown at the moment, terrified, stretched beyond ourselves, ashamed, realizing the future is in our hands. We must all do our work. Be accountable and go heal, simultaneously, continuously. It's never too late.

We will not cancel us. If we give up this strategy, we will learn together the other strategies that will ultimately help us break these cycles, liberate future generations from the burden of our shared and private pain, leaving nothing unspeakable in our bones, no shame in our dirt.

Each of us is precious. We, together, must break every cycle that makes us forget this.

AFTERWORD

Malkia Devich Cyril

I remember lying on a disheveled bed in the disheveled room of a fourteen-year-old in 1988, reading the now acclaimed book, edited by Cherríe Moraga and Gloria Anzaldúa, *This Bridge Called My Back*. I recall feeling exposed, like they knew the intimate violations that had rearranged my bones, and the bones of every Black woman and genderqueer person I knew, into a crossing over, a ladder that those in power would use to climb out from the hell they have made, a viaduct that everyone alive would use to traverse from history to the future. The aha moments that came when there was language to crystallize the multiple oppressed identities I walked with—Black, working class, queer, woman, butch/genderqueer—were lightning strikes in my life that woke me up simultaneously to a larger and deeper vision for justice. The writings in that book helped me begin to understand who I was and who I needed to be as an activist, an artist, and a social movement leader. It helped me to understand the many forms of violence patriarchy wages against all bodies, and particularly against the bodies of women, genderqueer, and transgender people. It was then, reading that book against the staccato violence of a burgeoning drug war, that I saw with crystal clarity that the violence in my body was a direct result of the violence done to me and mine.

See, I was afraid then, in the 1980s, just as my mother had been in the 1960s and 1970s. Afraid to be jumped in the street, chased, raped, beaten. By men I knew and loved, boys I didn't know, and homophobes across the gender spectrum. My mother and I both had good reason to be afraid, as did my sister, as do my nieces. As do you. My body wears scars like a memory. Just like my mother's. Just like yours. The world can be dangerous for people like us. For hearts like these. For many, that fear was a formative one that translated over time into a stance of aggressive victimology. Somebody knows what I mean. A powerlessness welded into a stance, a posture. A posture that, when it reached the eyes, became a lens, a lens through which a growing movement processed it's understanding of power through intellectual righteousness. Ask me how I know.

Since the 1980s, I've had the good fortune of steeping in all manner of radical feminist literature, Black radical writings, the perspectives of immigrants and Indigenous people on harm, on justice, and on accountability. Through my own personal healing, I have learned to recognize the difference between a situation that is genuinely unsafe and one that is simply uncomfortable. I have learned the difference between intolerable feelings and intolerable conditions. While none of this work has made me perfect, it has helped me to become a better abolitionist, one who recognizes that, while all harms are not the same, for a survivor like me, they might feel that way.

The hard part is that this triggered posture through which I have sometimes taken action is rarely effective against institutional enemies, or those individuals positioned to do the greatest harm. It rarely brings down CEOs and right-wing politicians. It doesn't tend to create new infrastructure for those who had been violated or new pathways for those who did the violating. Instead, it is most often aimed at those closest, those in greatest proximity to our wounds. It can be a painful way to live and an impossible way to build effective and accountable social movements.

But I believe we *can* build effective and accountable movements. We *can* tear down this system without destroying each other. With attention, intention, and practice, we can transform our understanding of accountability. Over many years, I've learned that accountability isn't something anyone can hold another to, it is something we can help each other be, within boundaries that keep us secure. Accountability isn't punishment, though it is frequently wielded as such. But, when we are able to discern between what our triggered bodies say and what our grounded bodies do, we can build the kinds of systems and practices we need to align our leadership and our movements. This is a spiritual alignment as much as it is a political one. It correlates principle and purpose to process and outcomes. It is not reactive. It is not punitive. It walks through the dystopia of the moment toward the world we want.

Though the digital age and a growing social media market make it hard to take the time required to transform triggered responses to grounded ones, we can still slow down.

Though the racial and economic hierarchies into which we were born and through which we are forcibly oppressed act negatively upon us every day, we can allow for principled hierarchies with consent as their character.

Though the leaders that govern our world have passed policies of deep harm, authorized actions that kill, and used the State to make so many stateless, pushing our traditional forms of collective governance into the shadows—we can conjure a new sense of belonging beyond the nation-state. We can make decisions together, build consensus together.

Though the intrusions and conflicts we have borne witness to for generations have resulted in military action or militarized families, we can heal. I promise you, even the harms that seem impossible, we can heal them.

Within a white supremacist justice system riddled with bias, a stalker state that watches but fails to protect, a system of brutal policing and mass incarceration that deforms familial relations, kinship ties, and community cohesion, and a patriarchy that reifies these dynamics of brokenness and does nothing to restore them to wholeness—asymmetrical tactics to confront those in power makes sense. As an abolitionist and as a survivor and as someone that has caused harm in the world as well as been a vector for healing, I have deep compassion for those who seek to use their voices to name harm rather than look to the criminal justice system.

I also reject the right-wing myth that in calling out harm, the Left proves itself intellectually rigid. I reject the idea that in our attempts to bypass a brutal criminal legal system by using our voice instead of the police, we have somehow moved from being defenders of dissidence to suppressors of speech. That is right-wing propaganda and white supremacy's lie. That is patriarchy's gaslighting and capitalism's violence. For criminal legal violations that cannot be entrusted to the law, asymmetrical responses like call outs are exactly right.

Yet, when we use mass or social media to manage conflicts that would never be judged by a criminal legal system, when it is used to focus not on sexual or physical assault but on political or creative differences, when it is a reaction infused with trauma, or an attempt to expose a leader for practices deemed unsavory but not illegal—we aren't debating, we aren't being accountable, and what was once a grain of truth becomes a field. We are separating from those we swore to protect. We are aiding and abetting the counter-intelligence forces that have successfully used visible rifts for years to destroy what we have built.

At the end of the day, forging the principles we need and the practices, people, institutions, and conditions we need to adhere to them—that has always been the heart of movement building to me. Being willing to acknowledge the breaking points without disavowing the broken pieces in your hands requires bravery. It requires great honesty to admit that innocence is an imagined narrative created to deny everyone agency, and to set up those who cross lines and cause harm as deviant outliers, exceptions to humanity's rule.

Especially when even a modest look inside one's own history reveals that every hand has dirt on it. Everyone has worked this earth as we have walked it. While all harms are not equal, even the most heinous require a way home.

I believe that's what we are all searching for: a way home. A path through this wilderness. But to walk through wilderness we must become more and more comfortable with what is wild in each of us. The contradictions, the ways suffering shapes who we are and how we organize. That's why our way forward isn't to dismiss call outs, or to urge people to stop. No, our words are powerful and are meant to be heard. The way forward is to forge abolition with both hands in the dirt, building empathy in the mirror; it's to remember that innocence is never a prerequisite for human dignity, nor for human rights and freedom; that the words we speak aloud offer a prediction for what will be, and must therefore manifest not our smallest vision for the world, but our biggest.

This Bridge Called My Back set me on the path to find my own natural wildness, the truth of my integrity that the world's violence tried to keep hidden from me. I feel especially lucky to bear witness as modern thought leaders like adrienne maree brown build upon the writings of other radical feminists of color speak with their whole heart to the cause of freedom for us all. Audre Lorde, one of my favorite radical feminists of color said it best,

> and when we speak we are afraid
> our words will not be heard
> nor welcomed
> but when we are silent
> we are still afraid
>
> So it is better to speak
> remembering
> we were never meant to survive.[1]

1   Audre Lorde, "A Litany for Survival," in *The Collected Poems of Audre Lorde* (New York: W. W. Norton & Company, 1997), 256.

RESOURCES

These are resources I currently refer people to around issues of transformative justice. Those listed here can refer and point you to more resources, and in the next few years several more books are coming on abolition, principled struggle, and transformative justice, so please see this list not as a definitive, finished offering, but as seeds for developing your own garden of resources.

Bay Area Transformative Justice Collective, particularly their Pod Mapping technology, batjc.wordpress.com.

adrienne maree brown, *Emergent Strategy: Shaping Change, Changing* Worlds (Chico, CA: AK Press, 2017).

The Critical Resistance website, particularly the resource section "Addressing Harm, Accountability, and Healing," criticalresistance.org.

Ejeris Dixon and Leah Lakshmi Piepzna-Samarasinha, *Beyond Survival: Strategies and Stories from the Transformative Justice Movement* (Chico, CA: AK Press, 2020).

Angela Y. Davis, *Are Prisons Obsolete?* (New York: Seven Stories Press, 2003).

Emergent Strategy Ideation Institute is working with BEAM (The Black Emotional and Mental Health Collective) on creating a directory of mediators willing to support BIPOC movement conflict, alliedmedia.org/speaker-projects/emergent-strategy-ideation-institute and www.beam.community.

Staci K. Haines, *The Politics of Trauma: Somatics, Healing, and Social Justice* (Berkeley: North Atlantic Books, 2019).

The work of Prentis Hemphill, particularly the *Finding Our Way* podcast and "Letting Go of Innocence," both available at prentishemphill.com.

Just Practice, "Steps to End Prisons & Policing: A Mixtape on Transformative Justice," just-practice.org/steps-to-end-prisons-policing-a-mix-tape-on-transformative-justice.

Mariame Kaba and Shira Hassan, *Fumbling Towards Repair: A Workbook for Community Accountability Facilitators* (Chicago: Self-Published, 2019), available through AK Press.

National Harm Reduction Coalition: Harm Reduction Principles, harmreduction.org/about-us/principles-of-harm-reduction.

National Queer and Trans Therapists of Color Network (NQTTCN), for people who need personal healing support beyond what movements can hold, nqttcn.com/.

Lama Rod Owens, *Love and Rage: The Path of Liberation through Anger* (Berkeley: North Atlantic Books, 2020).

Sarah Schulman, *Conflict is Not Abuse: Overstating Harm, Community Responsibility, and the Duty of Repair* (Vancouver: Arsenal Pulp Press, 2016).

Savannah Shange, *Progressive Dystopia: Abolition, Anti-Blackness, and Schooling in San Francisco* (Durham: Duke University Press, 2019).

Paul Stametz, *Mycelium Running: How Mushrooms Can Help Save the World* (Berkeley: Ten Speed Press, 2005).

Steven Universe, an animated television series created by Rebecca Sugar that continually addresses the pathway from trauma to healing in individual and collective settings.